Where Families Live

By Jenna Lee Gleisner

SPARKS

Picture Glossary

farmhouse   13

houseboat   9

hut 15

stilt house 11

A family lives here.

house

A family lives here.

apartment

A family lives here.

houseboat

A family lives here.

stilt house

A family lives here.

farmhouse

A family lives here.

hut

Do You Know?

This family lives in a _____.

house	apartment	houseboat
stilt house	farmhouse	hut